REBEL GIRLS

Little Library

10+ Women who Dance

This is a work of creative nonfiction. It is a collection of heartwarming and thought-provoking stories inspired by the lives and adventures of influential women. It is not an encyclopedic account of the events and accomplishments of their lives.

www.rebelgirls.com

Rebel Girls, Inc.
421 Elm Ave.
Larkspur, CA 94939

Text by Dinah Dunn
Art direction by Giulia Flamini
Graphic design by Kristen Brittain
Graphic design and additional illustrations: Alessandro Raimondo
Portrait illustrations: 4: Ana Juan, 8: Ana Juan,
12: Taylor McManus, 16: Juliette Toma, 20: Renike,
24: Ping Zhu, 28: Chaaya Prabhat, 32: Amy Phelps,
36: Rafaela Rijo-Núñez, 40: Eleni Debo

Printed in China, 2023
10 9 8 7 6 5 4 3 2 1
ISBN: 979-8-88964-077-6

FSC
www.fsc.org
MIX
Paper | Supporting responsible forestry
FSC™ C018179

CONTENTS

Alicia Alonso

Ballerina

December 21, 1920–October 17, 2019 | Cuba

Alicia was a young ballerina with a great career ahead of her when she got sick. Her illness made her slowly lose her eyesight.

To get better, Alicia had to have surgery. Then, she had to stay in bed for months without moving. She could not laugh or cry or move her head. But she still had to dance—in the only way she could.

"I danced in my mind," Alicia said. "Blinded, motionless, flat on my back, I taught myself to dance *Giselle*." She went through every movement of the famous ballet. Teachers came and sat by her bed. They talked her through the parts she couldn't imagine. In her mind, she was the prima ballerina—the star dancer.

Over time, her eyesight improved enough that she could get out of bed. One day, the American Ballet Theatre's prima ballerina got injured. They called Alicia to step in. She was already almost blind, but how could she say no? The ballet was *Giselle*!

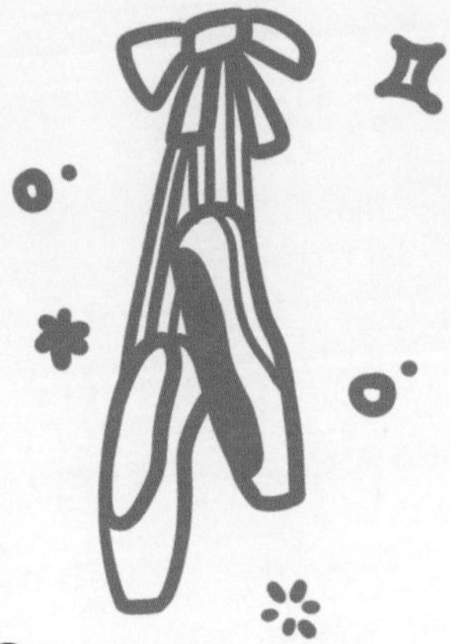

As soon as she started to dance, the audience fell in love. Alicia danced with grace. She worked with her partners so they would be exactly where she needed them. The spotlights were bright enough for her to see. She used them to figure out where she was on the stage.

Her style was so unique that she

was asked to dance all over the world. But her dream was to bring ballet to Cuba, her home country. Back from her travels, she taught ballet to Cuban dancers. She founded the Ballet Alicia Alonso company, which later became the Ballet Nacional de Cuba.

Alicia was named Cuba's prima ballerina *assoluta*. That was the highest honor in ballet. Just like she imagined all those years ago.

SCAN TO HEAR MORE!

Carmen Amaya

Dancer

Circa 1918–November 19, 1963 | Spain

On the night Carmen was born, Barcelona, Spain, was hit by a terrible storm. Thunder boomed, lightning crashed, and the rain turned the roads into rivers.

When Carmen's father first saw her dance, he wondered if the power of the storm had entered his daughter when she was born. Carmen learned flamenco from her aunt, who was herself a great dancer. Flamenco is a Spanish style of dance. It includes fast footwork, hand clapping, and finger snapping. A singer and a guitar player make the music.

To earn money for her family, Carmen danced barefoot in the restaurants down by the waterfront. Her dad would play the guitar.

A show-business manager saw Carmen's talent and offered to help her. When she was six years old, she began to perform in big theaters. She soon earned enough money for her family to move out of the shack where she was born.

Onstage, Carmen did not wear dresses like other women dancers. She liked to wear the tight pants and high-cut jackets that men wore for flamenco. When she first walked on stage like that, the audience was upset. How dare she wear men's clothing!

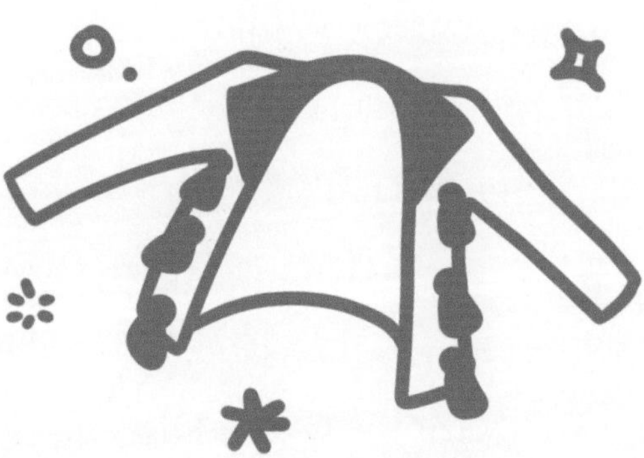

But when she began to

dance, Carmen stopped the talk. Stamping out lightning-fast beats on the stage, she sometimes broke the floorboards. She moved like no one had before.

Carmen's talent took her all over the world. She performed for the president of the United States and the Queen of England. And when she returned to Barcelona, the city built a fountain near where she was born. It showed children dancing and playing guitar, just like how Carmen began.

SCAN TO HEAR MORE!

Jalaiah Harmon

Dancer and Choreographer

Born August 28, 2005 | USA

Once there was a girl who got the whole world dancing. Jalaiah took classes in all kinds of dance: hip-hop, ballet, jazz, tap. She would spend hours putting together moves in fun dance routines.

One day after school, she made up a fast new dance to a song called "Lottery" by a rapper named K Camp. She swung her arms, popped her shoulders, spun her whole body, and bounced to the music. She filmed herself performing it and posted it on social media.

Buzz! Ping! Chirp! Jalaiah's phone blew up as the video was liked and shared. People around the world started trying to do Jalaiah's moves.

Her dance, known as the Renegade, soon made its way to TikTok.

Suddenly, professional dancers and celebrities were performing the Renegade. Every time Jalaiah opened the app, someone new was doing her dance. At 14, she had created one of the most viral dance trends ever!

This is exciting! she thought. But then she realized no one knew she had invented the dance. "I was upset," she said. "It wasn't fair."

Jalaiah decided to speak up. Whenever she saw someone online doing the Renegade, she wrote that she was the creator. Celebrities began to notice and support her.

When K Camp heard that she had created the dance, he got in touch with her. Together they recorded him rapping and her dancing, so more people would know what she did. "It's good that I influence other people," she said. "But I just like to dance."

JoJo Siwa

Singer and Dancer

Born May 19, 2003 | USA

From the time she could walk, JoJo was dancing in her mom's studio. She loved being onstage. And she loved to dress up. She had her own style full of glitter, hair bows, and lots of color!

JoJo's moves and style landed her a spot on the TV show *Dance Moms*. Her big laugh and charm quickly made her a fan favorite. On YouTube, JoJo created dance videos for those fans and found new ones. She also filmed silly videos. One time, she made a giant ice cream dessert. Another time, she covered her body in purple glitter.

But there was more to JoJo than just sweets and sparkles. She also asked kids everywhere to be kind to one another. She knows the world can be a difficult place. But if you have people around you who are good, she says, "then your world can be a good place."

Soon JoJo turned her love of dance, music, and all things fun into a full-time job. She started performing her own songs on tour. She also sold hair bows so fans could try her look.

As she grew up, JoJo shared her big life events with her fans. When she was 17, she told the world that she is gay. It was scary to come out, but she knew she had to be true to herself. "I want to be a role model for people who love love," she said.

JoJo continues to find ways to make people feel included. On the television show *Dancing with the Stars*, she was the first woman to dance with another woman. JoJo proves that a little girl with a lot of sparkle can make big dreams come true.

SCAN TO HEAR MORE!

Judith Jamison

Dancer and Choreographer

Born May 10, 1943 | USA

As a child, Judith could never sit still. She was always jumping and playing. She even crashed her first bicycle straight into a tree!

What will we do with all this wiggly energy? Judith's mom asked. She put Judith in ballet lessons when she was six. Judith loved moving her body through the steps and rhythms. She tried many styles of dance from all around the world. She danced through elementary school and high school and right into college.

One day, she went to see the Alvin Ailey American Dance Theater. She sat in the theater watching the smooth movements of the dancers. Judith thought, *I can do that*.

She decided to try out for the dance company, but it did not go well. She felt clunky and stiff. The flowing dances with the jazzy music were so different from the ballet she knew. She left the theater in tears. *I'm not good enough*, she thought.

But she was wrong. Three days later, Judith was asked to join the dance company. In time, she learned modern dance. For 15 years, she performed all over the world. Alvin Ailey created dances for her, including a famous solo called *Cry*.

Judith later worked on Broadway shows and started her own dance company. And when

Alvin decided not to run the company anymore, he asked Judith if she would take over. She became the first Black woman to direct a modern dance company.

Even after she stopped dancing and her bones felt achy, Judith couldn't sit still. "I've been in extraordinary motion my entire life," she says.

SCAN TO HEAR MORE!

Misty Copeland

Ballerina

Born September 10, 1982 | USA

The audience waited for Misty to step onstage. The ballet was called *The Firebird*. After more than 12 years of dancing, it was the first time Misty had danced as a prima ballerina. She was the first Black woman to have that role at the American Ballet Theatre.

All eyes were on her as the curtain rose. Her arms moved gracefully like the wings of a bird. She spun and soared across the stage in long, beautiful jumps. She was amazing.

When the final curtain fell, Misty let herself feel the pain. During the performance, she had broken her leg in six places. She needed surgery. The doctor told her she might never dance again.

No more dancing? Misty felt like her world had ended. She loved ballet too much to stop dancing. She had begun when she was 13 years old. At the time, she was living in a motel with her mom and her five siblings. As a child she was often homeless. Ballet made her feel safe and strong. Now she had found a way to have a career doing something she loved. She had to keep going. And she didn't want to let down all the Black people cheering her on.

So Misty went through the surgery, which added a steel plate to her leg. She worked through months of painful therapy. She trained so that she was strong again.

And she began to push back on

the idea that Black people did not belong in ballet. She did it when she danced the famous ballet *Swan Lake*. Some people thought she should paint herself white to play the white swan. But she didn't. She danced in her own beautiful skin.

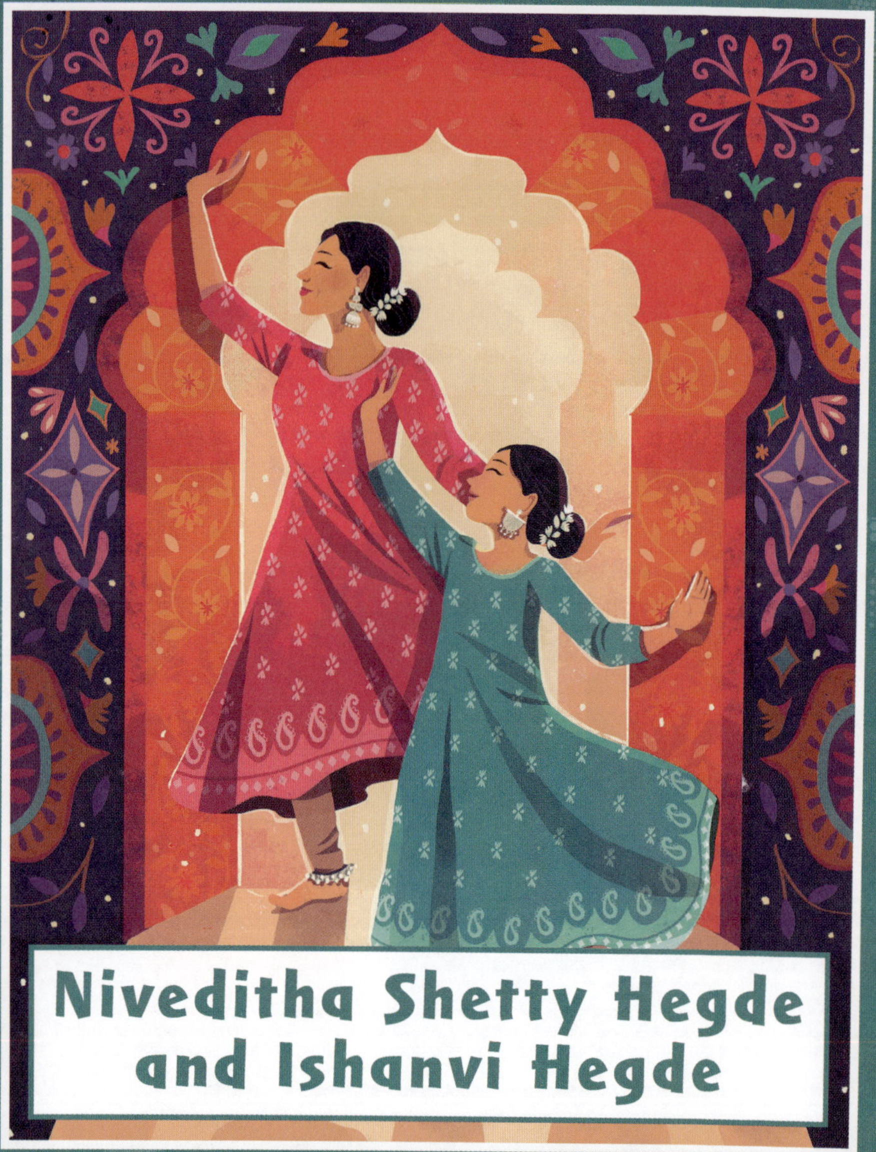

Niveditha Shetty Hegde and Ishanvi Hegde

Dancers

Niveditha, born June 12, 1984 | Ishanvi, born April 3, 2014
India and United Arab Emirates

Once there was a girl named Niveditha—Nivi for short—who loved watching her mom dance. Her arms moved like ocean waves. She kicked one leg high while standing on the other. And her mom hadn't even taken a class!

Nivi wanted to move and spin and swirl just like her mom. So her mother taught her everything she knew. Nivi had no idea that 30 years later, she'd be teaching her daughter, Ishanvi, how to dance too.

When Ishanvi was two, she started dancing along with songs on the radio. If Nivi danced, Ishanvi tried to follow her movements. So Nivi started showing Ishanvi how to do simple Indian dances. They had so much fun together! Soon they started making up their own moves.

Ishanvi's dad thought their routines were so cool he started filming them. Nivi posted a video online. It got more than 7.7 million views!

Nivi and Ishanvi now treat each dance number like a professional performance. Sometimes they dress up in matching saris, with *maang tikka* jewelry on their foreheads. Other times, they wear tanks tops and shorts and perform at the beach, the ocean waves dancing behind them. It is a lot of work, but Nivi and Ishanvi always enjoy themselves.

Sharing their videos with the world is fun. But Nivi and Ishanvi's favorite thing about creating new dances is doing it together. They love inspiring others to dance together too. Nivi said, "When I receive messages about how our dance lifts someone's spirits, I feel good that we started this."

Sherenté

Dancer and Activist

Born June 11, 2000 | USA and Narragansett

Once upon a time, a teenager named Sherenté put on a colorful shawl and began to dance. They stepped and twirled to the beat of a drum. To someone in the Narragansett tribe, it looked like a familiar dance. But it wasn't. It was a brave, one-of-a-kind performance.

Sherenté spent their childhood watching their elders dance in powwows. The dancers wore special outfits. Through dance, they told stories that have been handed down through their families.

Sherenté's father performed in Eastern War Dances, and their mother danced Fancy Shawl. At first, Sherenté danced the same style as their father, but it didn't feel right. They were more comfortable performing with the women.

Sherenté was Two-Spirit. LGBTQIA+ Indigenous people use this term for people who are not just "male" or "female."

A lot of the dances at powwows are contests. When Sherenté started Fancy Shawl dancing, some powwow officials were upset. Because Sherenté was Two-Spirit, some people thought they shouldn't be allowed to compete with the women. For more than a year, the judges refused to score Sherenté. Sherenté felt sad and alone. But they kept dancing.

Other people stood up for Sherenté. They thought the way powow officials treated Sherenté was wrong. They reminded the Narragansett people that the tribe was always accepting in the past. Finally, Sherenté's dances were scored. In time, they placed first!

Sherenté wanted people to know about the challenges Two-Spirit people face. Soon, a movie, *Being Thunder*, was made about Sherenté. It let them share their journey with the world. As Sherenté says, "No one can tell our stories better than us."

SCAN TO HEAR MORE!

Vitória Bueno

Ballerina

Born March 23, 2004 | Brazil

Once there was a girl who was always moving around. Before she even knew it, she was dancing.

Vitória was born without arms, but that didn't matter. As she says, "For me, arms, they're just a detail. I don't feel like I need them at all." Most people use their arms and hands to do the dishes or brush their teeth. But Vitória can do these things and more—using her feet!

One day, when Vitória was five years old, her doctor noticed the bounce in her step. It was clear she liked to dance.

Maybe you would like to give ballet a try? the doctor asked.

Vitória and ballet clicked right away. When she heard the *plink* of the piano, she was ready to go. Vitória moved her body to the music beautifully. When other girls raised their arms, she straightened her neck and tilted her head up. It felt like she was stretching toward the sky. She found she didn't really need arms to do the movements. She was a natural!

By the time she was 16, she was jumping and twirling on stages all over the world.

"I think I was born to dance," Vitória said. "I was born to dance ballet."

In 2021, she competed on the television show *America's Got*

Talent. She wore a beautiful white tutu and a sparkly crown. Her performance brought the judges and audience to their feet.

While Vitória did not win, *America's Got Talent* gave her a boost. "The show changed my life a lot," she said. "I was able to believe more in my potential."

Yoshiko Chuma

Choreographer and Performance Artist

Born December 25, 1950 | Japan and USA

When Yoshiko danced, anything could happen. She would leap around and stomp her boots on the floor—*boom, boom, boom!* Or she would leave the stage and walk around the theater. Maybe she would grab a chair and swing it over her head. Her performances were always different from anything audiences had seen before.

Yoshiko never took dance classes. As a girl in Osaka, Japan, Yoshiko felt like she didn't fit in. In college a friend told her about a place with artists from all over the world: New York City. That's where Yoshiko decided to go. She did not speak English, but when she danced, she felt like she was talking with her body.

Yoshiko started her own dance company. She named it the School of Hard Knocks. That means learning things out in the real world, the way Yoshiko did, instead of in a classroom.

The School of Hard Knocks performances are a mix of modern dance, film, art, music, and more. The dancers have performed everywhere, from streets to concert halls to cozy living rooms. Sometimes audiences are confused. They never know what is going to happen next. Yoshiko likes it that way.

Yoshiko and her dance company have won many awards. She has traveled to more than 50 countries and worked with more than 1,500 people to create her unique works of art. She has never stopped looking for her next inspiration. She said, “Sometimes I don’t know the difference between my art and my life.”

About Rebel Girls

Rebel Girls is a global, multi-platform empowerment brand dedicated to helping raise the most inspired and confident generation of girls through content, experiences, products, and community. Originating from an international best-selling children's book, Rebel Girls amplifies stories of real-life women throughout history, geography, and field of excellence. With a growing community of nearly 20 million self-identified Rebel Girls spanning more than 100 countries, the brand engages with Generation Alpha through its book series, award-winning podcast, events, and merchandise. With the 2021 launch of the Rebel Girls app, the company has created a flagship destination for girls to explore a wondrous world filled with inspiring true stories of extraordinary women.

As a B Corp, we're part of a global community of businesses that meet high standards of social and environmental impact.

Join the Rebel Girls community:

Facebook: facebook.com/rebelgirls
Instagram: @rebelgirls
Twitter: @rebelgirlsbook
TikTok: @rebelgirlsbook
Web: rebelgirls.com
Podcast: rebelgirls.com/podcast
App: rebelgirls.com/audio

If you liked this book, please take a moment to review it wherever you prefer!